PORN
NATION

DISCUSSION GUIDE

PORN NATION

DISCUSSION GUIDE

MICHAEL LEAHY
With **RICK JAMES**

NORTHFIELD PUBLISHING
Chicago

Published in association with the literary agency of Sanford Communication, Inc., Portland, Oregon.
Cover Design: The DesignWorks Group
Cover Image: Jeff Miller / The DesignWorks Group
Interior Design: Smartt Guys design
Editor: Christopher Reese

Library of Congress Cataloging-in-Publication Data

Leahy, Michael.
 Porn nation discussion guide / Michael Leahy.
  p. cm.
 ISBN 978-0-8024-8127-6
  1. Pornography--United States. 2. Internet pornography--United States. 3. Sex in mass media--United States. I. Title.
 HQ472.U6L43 2008
 176'.70973--dc22
       2007048919

ISBN-10: 0-8024-8127-2
ISBN-13: 978-0-8024-8127-6

We hope you enjoy this book from Northfield Publishing. Our goal is to provide high-quality, thought-provoking books and products that connect truth to your real needs and challenges. For more information on other books and products written and produced from a biblical perspective, go to www.moodypublishers.com or write to:

Northfield Publishing
820 N. LaSalle Boulevard
Chicago, IL 60610

1 3 5 7 9 10 8 6 4 2

Printed in the United States of America

CONTENTS

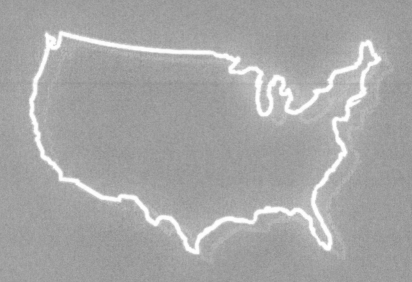

ABOUT THE AUTHORS

Michael Leahy is a recovering sex addict and the founder and executive director of BraveHearts, an organization dedicated to increasing the public's awareness of the hidden dangers and long-term consequences of pornography consumption. Before launching BraveHearts in 2003, Michael was a sales executive in the computer industry and worked for companies like IBM, Unisys, and NEC. Michael is the father of two boys; his first marriage ended in divorce in 1998 after his thirty-year relationship with pornography escalated into a self-destructive sexual addiction.

Now ten years into recovery, Michael has appeared on numerous national television programs like ABC's 20/20 and *The View* and in major media publications such as *USA Today* as an expert on the subjects of pornography, sexual addiction, and the impact sex in media is having on our culture. He's shared his compelling story and expertise in churches, at conferences, and with over 40,000 students on more than one hundred campuses worldwide in his critically acclaimed multimedia presentation "Porn Nation: The Naked Truth." Michael is remarried and currently resides with his wife, Christine, in the Washington, D.C. area.

Rick James, coauthor of this special discussion guide for use with *Porn Nation*, is a gifted writer and communicator. He is the publisher of CruPress, a popular national speaker for Campus Crusade for Christ, and author of the recent book *Jesus Without Religion* (InterVarsity Press, 2007). A graduate of Trinity Evangelical Divinity School (M.Div.), Rick was an art director at the New York ad agency of Young & Rubicam before joining Campus Crusade. He and his wife, Katie, have three children and currently reside in West Chester, Pennsylvania.

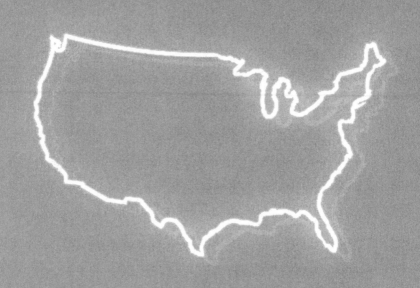

INTRODUCTION

There has always been a firewall between the world of commercial sex, and our clothed and sheltered society. While Adultworld has existed as long as civilization, you always had to come out of hiding in order to get there: on the other side of town, in unsanitary convenience stores, quarantined video aisles, or disease-infested red-light districts. You were exposed. You had to cross the Maginot Line of self-respect to put your purchase on the counter, under surveillance of camera, clerk, and other consumers. But the Internet changed that. The Internet changed everything. Now that world is accessed from a safe and sanitary distance, or at least we think so. As the headlines attest, there's really no such thing as anonymous sex. Someone's always left unprotected.

So you get a phone call from your sister-in-law with the surprising news that her husband, your brother, just announced he's leaving her and the kids for someone he met online. Or maybe she's the one who's leaving him for another man. Perhaps the stunning announcement was that of a longtime friend who's just been arrested and charged for soliciting sex with a minor. Or maybe the newsflash hits closer to home and you're reeling over your discovery of dozens of pornographic images and videos sitting on the family computer's hard drive: graphic titles and raunchy file names—unthinkably the property of some family member. Still closer to home, you may have even shocked yourself, compulsively following a striptease of links, unable to go for more than a few days or weeks without the rushing high that's served along with the online encounters.

And now it's personal, intimately personal. It's no longer out there;

it's moved home. We're networked to it, and it's networked together (voyeurism, exhibitionism, S&M, group sex—even child porn, bestiality, and images from real-life captives to human sex trafficking: each a small division of the larger sex industry). We no longer have the luxury to ignore it. Unlike famine, it refused to stay in its separate hemisphere. Speaking as one who's been both the user and the abused, I have spent years wondering who's to blame, wondering how we got here. Like cigarettes, hypersexuality (from Howard Stern to kiddie porn, and all that lies between) became part of our national lifestyle overnight, and was passed on to us without so much as a warning label for nursing mothers. But I'm not so concerned with questions of blame as I am about questions of truth. The truth about my issues, and the truth about our issues as a culture. And we both have issues.

It was only after losing everything that mattered to me—my fifteen-year marriage, my family of two boys, my home, my job, most of my friends, and my reputation—that I finally hit bottom and began looking for answers.

That was ten years ago. Since then I have been on the long road of recovery and, thank God, it's been a successful journey. Having a decade to do little more than process how I got here, I have asked a lot of questions. Some of those questions are contained in this discussion guide. I believe talking about these issues now is a lot better than talking about them later in a recovery group, because you never saw what was coming.

Most of the questions are opened ended, meaning I want you to think about them as I have, and come to your own conclusions; this is a discussion, after all, not a test for right answers. Talking through these issues will promote self-discovery and, hopefully, shine some rays of hope. Not a cultural utopian hope played to John Lennon's "Imagine," but a personal, redemptive hope: that anyone who wants to be free can be; that anyone who wants to be whole will be; that anyone who wants forgiveness will receive it.

—MICHAEL LEAHY

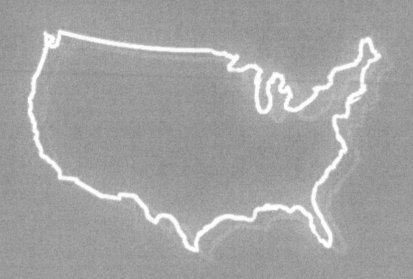

DISCUSSION GUIDE

PORN COMES OF AGE

Before porn could be stashed in tidy folders far down in the subdirectory of a computer, people actually had to physically hide their porn. It's true. And we used to have to walk five miles to school, listen to record albums, and change the TV channels without a remote. Yes, these were the pioneering days of porn, and I'd find pictures of naked women in the strangest of places. In the bathroom at a friend's house. In the woods, hidden under old pieces of plywood. In piles of trash. Whenever I'd come across these pictures, I would just stare, silently inhaling the images, taking them in to every cell of my being and locking them there. In the magazines, the pictures didn't just show women naked from the waist up. Unlike the black-and-white images on the deck of playing cards, these pictures were in color—glorious 1970s color—before photographers had isolated the gene for oversaturation.

Most of the time I found *Playboy* magazines, but occasionally I'd stumble across some really weird stuff with men and women, I assumed, having sex. I'd heard about sex before, but no one had ever sat down and explained it to me. The magazines made it look dirty, sometimes downright disgusting. The only sex education I'd had up to that point was a special night class that I attended, at school, with my father, taught by a priest. As I think about it, this was probably an effective way to teach abstinence, even lifelong celibacy.

So that was the extent of my formal and informal sex education. Looking at all of those pictures was exciting, but I still didn't know what to do with that newfound sexual energy. But then, as most of us do, I found out... all by myself.

Throughout junior high, suffice it to say that being sent to my room was no longer a punishment. I sent myself. That's how I learned to cope with the angst of stress, pressure, boredom, frustration, Mondays, bad hair days, and the absence of Oreos in the pantry. It was a cure-all more versatile than aspirin. Unfortunately, it didn't resolve any of the real issues; it was simply a pacifier that I would refuse to grow out of.

—Michael Leahy, *Porn Nation: The Naked Truth*

DISCUSS

1. For me, pornography and sex became a coping mechanism for dealing with negative feelings. Is this really a problem, or is it just normal?

2. I found out about sex primarily from porn and peers. Though I'm sure they tried, my parents really didn't factor into it. How did you learn about sex?

3. Do you think porn serves any role in sex education? Why or why not?

4. What might be some of the harmful messages implicit in porn, especially for adolescents learning about sex?

5. In my Porn Nation presentations, I share, with no small amount of embarrassment, some of my defining and formative sexual experiences. What events or experiences have shaped you and your views about sex?

6. For me, college life was like "throwing gas on the fire" of my growing addiction. How has college life changed your views and practices concerning sex?

7. Like many kids, I stumbled upon pornographic material that had been hidden by adults. How would you feel if you found porn on your parents' computer? Why?

8. Have your parents ever done anything in the sexual area that has disappointed or hurt you?

9. Do you ever experience guilt or shame related to any past sexual experience? If you could erase any sexual event or experience, what would it be?

10. When you were young, do you feel you were adequately protected from negative sexual experiences or influences like porn?

11. To the frustration of some, I'm sure, I bring God into the Porn Nation discussion. He is, after all, relevant to any moral or spiritual discussion, and I feel sex involves both. Which of the following would you say is true (discuss your answer)?

God likes porn—God created sex and is glad we are having fun with it.

God does not care about porn—it's not a big deal as long as we are not hurting others.

God does not like porn—God created sex and is saddened by the abuse and exploitation of it.

God is pretty old-fashioned and is not aware of the Internet.

12. As they relate to God, which of these thoughts brings you the most comfort (discuss your answer)?

God isn't there, and we are free to do whatever we want sexually.

God is there and will forgive us for our failures in the sexual area.

God is there and will ultimately judge all evil.

God is there and will lead me in finding a person to truly love.

God is there, and he's like Morgan Freeman.

REFLECTION

For those interested, to understand God's heart in relation to marriage and sex, it would be helpful between now and next week to read over part of Jesus' Sermon on the Mount found in the gospel of Matthew, chapter 5.

MARRIED TO PORN

Adopting the Las Vegas axiom "What happens here, stays here," I decided not to go into great detail about my sexual past with my wife, Patty, and I never told her about my affinity for pornography. I convinced myself that we were a good match and that our sexual past wasn't important. Plus, I reasoned, *once we're married I won't want to look at that stuff anymore.* Somehow, I just knew that my lust for the material would magically go away once we started having regular bedroom sex as husband and wife. But just to make sure, right before I asked her to marry me, I took a trip to a place called Hedonism with a couple of my friends for a final sex binge. Let's just say that the resort lived up to its name, and leave it there. My goal was to get it all out of my system so that I would be ready to settle down to a wife and, hopefully, a family of my own. Funny how feeding your addictions in no way gets them out of your system—funny.

But the first clue suggesting my past was not getting boxed up along with my bachelor furnishings came no sooner than our wedding night. While Patty and I were hanging out in the lobby of the hotel, I started having a few drinks with my family and friends. As the night wore on, I started noticing the other women in the lobby, drinking in images as I used to with pornography. Part of "drinking in images" involved undressing them with my mind, followed by imagining myself having sex with them. It's a form of mental rape and is sexually arousing in a way that can hardly be detected by anyone else. It was a way of feeding myself lustful thoughts to fantasize on later.

So here I was on my wedding day, Patty all dressed in white, yet all I could think of was having sex with some of the bridesmaids and barflies at the hotel pub. Later that night, when we were finally alone, I would tell her that I was too tired from the busy day, then roll over and fall asleep. I never gave a second thought to what this night meant to her, and what kind of memories she would hold on to from that day. In retrospect it was ironically poetic: as the wedding night is the unveiling of one's spouse, Patty had gotten to see the real me as well as a trailer for the next decade and a half of our marriage. Nearly fifteen years would pass before we would ever talk to each other about what didn't happen on our wedding night and many other nights to follow.

—Michael Leahy, *Porn Nation: The Naked Truth*

DISCUSS

1. What do you believe that people are looking for in relationships?

2. What is the healthiest dating/marriage relationship you have ever personally observed? What made it "healthy"?

3. What was the worst relationship you ever had? What made it so horrible? Why did it fail?

4. Do you believe men and women are looking for different things in relationships? If so, what are the differences?

5. Do you think casual sex affects the self-esteem of men differently than women? How about the experience of jealousy and guilt?

6. My first wife, Patty, was not aware of my problem going into our marriage. Do you think you could marry a person knowing they struggle with porn or sexual addiction? What *would* be a "deal breaker" for you?

7. Would it be a problem for you to find out that your spouse had had many sexual partners before you?

8. In your mind, are there any circumstances that justify marital unfaithfulness?

9. Divorce rates hover around 50 percent. What do you think are the major reasons for this? Do you believe you will be married to the same person your whole life?

10. What do you think is most important to a successful marriage (rank in order and discuss)?

 — Friendship and compatibility
 — Sexual attraction and satisfaction
 — Sharing the same spiritual and moral values
 — Having things in common
 — Good communication

11. Again, it is difficult for me to separate God from sex and relationships. Do you think that God (discuss):

   — Has someone specific for you to marry?
   — Is irrelevant to your relationships?
   — Isn't concerned with who you marry as long as you love them?
   — Makes His will known through the search engines of eHarmony?

12. For those of you who do, why do you believe that God created sex? Marriage?

Many assume they know what the New Testament says about sex, but have never actually read it for themselves. So here, take a read:
> It is God's will that you should . . . avoid sexual immorality; that each of you should learn to control his own body in a way that is . . . honorable, not in passionate lust like [those] who do not know God; and that in this matter no one should wrong his brother or take advantage of him. (1 Thessalonians 4:3–6)

13. Do you think this is unreasonable or out of date? Why would sexual immorality be something that wrongs or takes advantage of someone else?

REFLECT

As relationships can move quickly in unplanned directions, it's important to give thought beforehand to some of the issues raised in this discussion. Between now and next week, on the page below, write out your beliefs, desires, and convictions as they relate to marriage and dating.

Marriage and Dating

Beliefs (what do I believe about marriage and dating?):

_____

_____

_____

_____

_____

_____

_____

_____

Desires (what is it I am truly looking for in a relationship?):

_____

_____

_____

_____

_____

_____

Convictions (no matter what, I will not cross these lines):

_____

_____

_____

_____

_____

_____

_____

_____

_____

_____

GENERATION SEX

The more time I had to myself, whether employed or not so employed, the more time I spent looking at porn. Now, fast access was becoming available at home, and I was the first to get it. But a new twist was added to my addiction. Just as Pepsi and Coke boost sales by adding diversity to their product line (Pepsi Light, Pepsi Lime, Pepsi Free, Pepsi Vanilla), so do the international manufacturers of porn. And as the number of pornographic sites proliferated, market niches multiplied like rabbits, offering porn in a starburst of flavors. Curious, and growing bored of Porn Light and Diet Porn, I started sampling the new brands. Stuff I had only heard of, or never even knew existed—girl on girl, lots of girls on lots of guys, BDS&M, web cams—so much to choose from.

One in particular, voyeurism, caught and captured my attention. I don't know exactly why. Whatever the reason, I would spend hours jumping from site to site, page to page, looking at hidden camera images of unsuspecting women.

This particular genre of porn created a greater level of sexual stimulation for me. Somehow a hierarchy gets established in the mind; it was, for example, more stimulating for me to see hidden camera shots of unsuspecting women than it was looking at pictures of group sex, which was more arousing than couple sex, which was more exciting than pictures of a naked woman, which—if we need to continue the regression—was more exciting than Marge Simpson in tennis shorts, and on and on. Eventually you get to a point where "normal" pictures and videos of naked women just don't do it for you anymore—it's warm, caffeine-free, diet Porn. But whenever I used these edgier images, my sexual arousal and the resulting climax were far more intense. Pavlovian dog that I had become, once I figured out how to get this "higher high," I spent more and more time salivating over increasingly debase forms of pornography. The more disturbing the image, the more I had to separate my emotions from what I was looking at, and the more I had to view women as objects instead of people. That was the only way I could reconcile what I was doing with these images in my mind with how I saw myself—or wanted other people to see me.

—Michael Leahy, *Porn Nation: The Naked Truth*

DISCUSS

1. How have you noticed sexual attitudes changing just in your own lifetime?

2. Do you have any concerns about what the next twenty years may bring in the sexual climate of our culture?

3. In what ways have you seen the effects of our increasingly sexualized culture on today's adolescents, perhaps even a brother or sister?

4. Along these lines, who do you think is the most, and least, helpful as far as cultural role models go?

5. In the current sexual climate how is a person perceived whose conviction is to wait for marriage before having sex?

6. Does the word *virgin* have the same connotations with women as it does men?

7. In your own thinking, what is wrong with an adolescent (say ages 10–13) having sex?

8. Studies indicate that many teens only consider intercourse to be sex, and nothing else. Is this your perspective? What makes sex, sex?

9. Do you think porn objectifies women? If so, why do you think women participate in it?

10. In *Porn Nation* I refer to porn's wide variety of genres (S&M, bondage, bestiality, voyeurism, group sex, child pornography, amateur/reality, etc.). How do you draw a line between what is personal preference and what is mental/moral deviancy?

11. As I mention in *Porn Nation*, voyeurism held a particular fascination for me. Many people have similar sexual fetishes or preferences.

Where do you think these fetishes come from? After prolonged use of porn, many gravitate toward such deviations. Why?

12. What sorts of difficulties might you encounter in trying to censor pornography in our society? Should we pass laws against it?

13. Every culture has general beliefs about sex that influence everything from media to fashion. List some of those unspoken beliefs that our culture has about sex.

14. How do these subtle messages affect you?

15. How do you honestly feel about raising your children in the current sexual environment? What scares you the most?

REFLECT

Springboarding from this discussion, as you go about your week, look to observe the degree of sexualization you see around you. Reflect on the ways this does and does not affect or influence you.

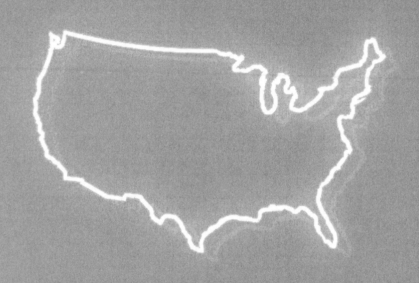

SEX SYNDROME

From the studies, it is apparent that many teens believe intercourse is the only thing that constitutes sex and that other sexual activities do not really count (kind of like ripping off only one flag in a game of flag football), and so any additional beliefs and pressures will all scaffold atop an already shaky foundation of thought.

As the game of Jenga continues, you have to stack on top social variables such as peer pressure. The Kaiser Family Foundation found 60% of teens cited "many of their friends had already done it" as a factor influencing their decision to have sex.

It's beginning to get a little wobbly, but we now need to heap upon it the weight of media, causing the whole structure to tremble with the blaring message that women need to be sexy or sexual enough in order to get the guy. Fifty-nine percent of girls age 12–19 agree that society tells them that attracting boys and acting sexy is one of the most important things teen girls can do.

There are, of course, always personal and societal barriers that act as drag on cultural change and hinder its rather deliberate speed. And this is perhaps where pornography plays its most significant role, lending Orwellian right-think media support to the sexual insurgency: changing attitudes of what's acceptable, causing passions to overflow their boundaries, sanding down inhibitions, and inciting the overthrow of restraint.

So the tower is beginning to crumble, but that shouldn't stop us from adding the last straw. What of a teen's psychological needs for acceptance and love, especially if the cupboards are bare at home? While the amount of psychological pressure varies from person to person and relationship to relationship, there is always some degree of pressure on women to act out sexually for the sake of impressing, pleasing, or keeping their boyfriends.

And that is how change happens and why cultural prophets are all too often narrow-minded in their laments, blaming it all on the media, or all on dysfunctional families, or all on peer pressure. The witch hunt is doomed from the start, as it is only hunting for a single witch. Cause and effect is as constant as gravity. But the relationship between causes and effects is often as complex as we find it in nature. It is not one thing, but the interplay of many things, eventually reaching a threshold . . . and then the winds change.

—Michael Leahy, *Porn Nation: The Naked Truth*

DISCUSS

1. What if someone you were involved with had an "addiction" to sex or pornography? What would you do? How would you respond?

2. I coined the term "Sex Syndrome" to describe the process preceding and leading up to sexual addiction. How would you know if you or someone close to you were in the beginning stages of Sex Syndrome?

3. Compulsion is feeling the need to do something you don't really want to do. Have you ever felt this compulsion in regard to sex? In regard to porn on the Internet?

4. Looking back on my path to addiction, I remember "crossing lines." Have you ever felt that sexually you crossed a line you had drawn for yourself, something you told yourself you would never do?

5. What makes porn addictive?

6. How do you know when a habit has turned into an addiction?

7. It is often shame and guilt that make people reluctant to share about addictions. What is the difference between shame and guilt? Have you struggled with either?

8. The current number of those addicted to sex and porn in the United States is roughly 15 million. Is this number surprisingly high or surprisingly low?

9. Do you think some people have a greater propensity toward sexual addiction than others?

10. Do you think the label of "sex addict" becomes an excuse for not accepting responsibility?

11. Why do so many 12-step programs seem to involve God or a higher power? What is the link between God and addiction?

12. Do you think prayer works? Have you ever experienced a time when you felt your prayers were specifically answered?

13. While far from a zealot, I do feel I have a strong relationship with God. How would you describe your spiritual life?

14. Obviously, my life had a significant turning point spiritually. What has been your spiritual experience or your spiritual story?

REFLECT

How *does* God influence your life: your choices, decisions, commitments—your day-to-day life? Over the course of the week, reflect on the nature or state of your relationship with God. For further reflection, consider these ancient proverbs found in the Old Testament and traditionally attributed to King Solomon. Having 6,000 concubines, we must consider the likelihood that Solomon struggled with his own sexual addiction. At any rate, he speaks from greater experience than you or I. Ponder and write down any thoughts or insights that come to mind from these proverbs.

Proverbs 5:7–14

"Now then, my sons, listen to me; do not turn aside from what I say. Keep to a path far from her, do not go near the door of her house, lest you give your best strength to others and your years to one who is cruel, lest strangers feast on your wealth and your toil enrich another man's house. At the end of your life you will groan, when your flesh and body are spent. You will say, "How I hated discipline! How my heart spurned correction! I would not obey my teachers or listen to my instructors. I have come to the brink of utter ruin in the midst of the whole assembly."

Proverbs 5:15–23

"Drink water from your own cistern, running water from your own well. Should your springs overflow in the streets, your streams of water in the public squares? Let them be yours alone, never to be shared with strangers. May your fountain be blessed, and may you rejoice in the wife of your youth. A loving doe, a graceful deer— may her breasts satisfy you always, may you ever be captivated by her love. Why be captivated, my son, by an adulteress? Why embrace the bosom of another man's wife? For a man's ways are in full view of the Lord, and he examines all his paths. The evil deeds of a wicked man ensnare him; the cords of his sin hold him fast. He will die for lack of discipline, led astray by his own great folly."

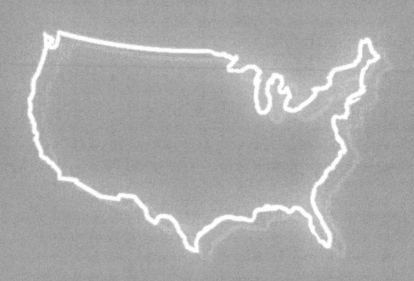

WHICH WAY TO REDEMPTION?

To escape moral guilt, typically, people turn to religion. But what I've found, as have many addicts, is that religion doesn't provide redemption, only the *possibility* or *path* to redemption. Certain activities are required, and if you choose an Eastern version, certain lifetimes are required. But that which we seek—forgiveness and acceptance before God—is elusive. Have we done enough? What is the criterion or cut off point—1,467 good deeds? What if we're one short? Is it just our actions that matter, or are motivations and thoughts important as well? Will a pilgrimage be required? Please—dear God—will someone tell us the requirements! The result, especially for the addict, is that religion simply heaps guilt upon us, laying out qualifying standards that we have no hope of ever meeting.

As addicts, we're already in a cycle of guilt and failure; religion just makes it worse, much worse. In the moral classroom we are a D student being promised redemption and forgiveness if we can get an A—but if we could get an A we wouldn't need redemption and forgiveness! Can someone—anyone—get us off of this Ferris wheel?

And then into the universe enters grace: true redemption and not simply the promise of it. In Jesus Christ, God does for us what we could never do for ourselves—dying for our sins and applying to us His perfect life. Bono, famed musician and humanitarian, puts it this way:

> You see, at the center of all religions is the idea of Karma. You know, what you put out comes back to you: an eye for an eye, a tooth for a tooth.... It's clear to me that Karma is at the very heart of the universe. I'm absolutely sure of it. And yet, along comes this idea called Grace to upend all that "as you reap, so you will

sow" stuff. Grace defies reason and logic. Love interrupts, if you like, the consequences of your actions, which in my case is very good news indeed, because I've done a lot of stupid stuff....

I'd be in big trouble if Karma was going to finally be my judge. It doesn't excuse my mistakes, but I'm holding out for Grace. I'm holding out that Jesus took my sins onto the Cross.... The point of the death of Christ is that Christ took on the sins of the world, so that what we put out did not come back to us, and that our sinful nature does not reap the obvious death. That's the point. It should keep us humbled.... It's not our own good works that get us through the gates of heaven. (From Michka Assayas, *Bono: In Conversation with Michka Assayas* [New York: Riverhead, 2005])

—Michael Leahy, *Porn Nation: The Naked Truth*

DISCUSS

1. In *Porn Nation* I state that while religion can generate guilt, grace releases us from it. How can religion impart guilt? Have you experienced this?

2. What is the prescription for sin that religion typically provides us with?

3. Why would religion rob us of hope rather than provide it, especially for the addict?

4. I state that religion provides a path or road to redemption but not redemption itself. What am I trying to get at?

5. Did your religious training and experience include any discussion about sex and relationships?

6. In what way is Jesus a manifestation of grace and not religion?

7. I see now that the standards for sex provided in Scripture were not meant to diminish our experience but to protect it and provide it with the healthiest context. How is it possible to see God's protection and provision in keeping sex within the boundaries of marriage?

8. Part of the 12-step credo states: God does for us what we could never do for ourselves. How is Christ's death a manifestation of this? What does He *do* for us?

9. Consider the following interaction between Jesus and someone severely afflicted:

"One who was there had been an invalid for thirty-eight years. When Jesus saw him lying there and learned that he had been in this condition for a long time, he asked him, 'Do you want to get well?'" (John 5:5–6)

The answer to Jesus' question seems obvious, so why would Jesus ask him if he really wanted to get well?

10. If you could be spiritually and sexually whole, but that meant changing your lifestyle or habits, would you still want to be well? (Think about it carefully.)

11. Write down on a piece of paper everything that you would want to be forgiven from in the sexual area, as well as any other area of your life.

REFLECT

I need you to decide what you want to do with what's on the paper. The Scriptures liken the decision to receive Christ to that of a marriage decision: a one-time choice to say, "I do." My decision to accept Christ and His forgiveness was expressed in a prayer similar to the one I've written below. If you have never made that decision, I invite you to make it, and then I invite you to rip up that damning piece of paper. You are certainly free not to make that decision; but I honestly don't know what to tell you about getting rid of what's on that paper.

Jesus, I want to know You. I want You to forgive my sins, everything I've done to hurt You and hurt others. I want You to change and direct my life. I want eternal life, and I believe You can do all of these things—that You will do all of these things. Thank You for dying for my sins, and I invite You into my life, for now, forever. Amen.

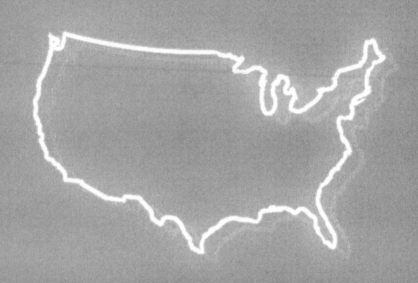

NEXT STEPS, RESOURCES, DISCUSSION LEADERS' GUIDE

NEXT STEPS
Spiritual Steps

While certainly qualified to share the story of my own redemption with you, I am not a minister. If you made the decision to invite Christ into your life, I would suggest getting connected to a church in your community, and if you're a college student I would also suggest connecting with a campus ministry like Campus Crusade for Christ, InterVarsity, Navigators, Fellowship of Christian Athletes, or another reputable organization that might be on your campus.

As an easy first step, I've found the website everystudent.com to be very helpful in answering basic questions about God and spiritual growth. I'd also suggest the Gospels (Matthew, Mark, Luke, John) as a good place to begin reading in the Bible. These four books recount the historical events of Jesus' life and message.

Whatever you do, remember that if you made the decision to invite Christ into your life: You have redemption—not just the hope of it—and the forgiveness of all your sins (Colossians 1:14); you have eternal life, and began a relationship with God that will never end (John 5:24); Christ has entered your life, indwells you, and under no circumstances will He ever leave you or abandon you (Hebrews 13:5).

I hope that's comforting to you and instills you with life and hope, as it has me.

Porn Nation

While this discussion booklet contains quotes from my story, I would encourage you to read *Porn Nation: The Naked Truth* in its entirety. I think there is much in my own journey that may help you in yours.

Small Group Resources

For further study on this topic after completing this discussion booklet, I suggest moving on to the seven-week topical studies found in the books *Flesh* (for men) and *Fantasy* (for women). These studies will lead the group through the essential issues and principles of spiritual growth that surround sex, lust, and pornography. Subjects covered include temptation and trials; truth and Scripture; experiencing God's forgiveness; the power of the Holy Spirit; community and accountability; God's purpose and plan for sex; and purity and prayer.

To order *Flesh* and *Fantasy* visit crupress.com or call 1-800-827-2788.

RECOVERY RESOURCES*

Sexual Addiction Twelve-Step Groups

Sexaholics Anonymous (SA)
PO Box 3565
Brentwood, TN 37024
Website: www.sa.org
Phone: 615-370-6062

Sex Addicts Anonymous (SAA)

ISO of SAA

PO Box 70949

Houston, TX 77270

Website: www.saa-recovery.org

Phone: 713-869-4902

Faith-based Recovery Groups

Celebrate Recovery

25422 Trabuco Rd #105-151

Lake Forest, CA 92630

Website: www.celebraterecovery.com

Phone: 949-581-0548

Bethesda Workshops

3710 Franklin Rd

Nashville, TN 37204

Website: www.bethesdaworkshops.org

E-mail: mferree@bethesdaworkshops.org

Phone: 866-464-4325

L.I.F.E. Ministries/LIFE Groups

PO Box 952317

Lake Mary, FL 32795

Website: www.freedomeveryday.org

Phone: 866-408-LIFE

Internet Filtering and Accountability Tools

Covenant Eyes

1525 West King St

Owosso, MI 48867

Website: www.covenanteyes.com

Phone: 877-479-1119

Net Nanny

2369 West Orton Cir

Salt Lake City, UT 84119

Website: www.netnanny.com

Phone: 801-977-7777

Bsafe Online

PO Box 1819

Bristol, TN 37621

Website: www.bsafehome.com

Phone: 850-362-4310

Pure Online

660 Preston Forest Center

Dallas, TX 75230

Website: www.pureonline.com

Phone: 214-580-2000

Other Helpful Resources

Brave Hearts

www.bravehearts.net

Porn Nation

www.pornnation.org

Online Sexual Addiction Screening Test Call

www.mysexsurvey.com

SexHelp.com

www.sexhelp.com

* All websites and phone numbers are accurate at the time of publication but may change in the future or cease to exist. The listing of website references and resources does not imply publisher endorsement of the site's entire contents. Groups and organizations are listed for informational purposes, and listing does not imply publisher endorsement of their activities.

RECOMMENDED READING

Porn Nation: Conquering America's #1 Addiction, Michael Leahy, Moody Publishers, 2008

Porn Nation: The Naked Truth, Michael Leahy, Moody Publishers, 2008

False Intimacy: Understanding the Struggle of Sexual Addiction, Dr. Harry Schaumburg, NavPress, 1997

The Purity Principle, Randy Alcorn, Multnomah, 2003

Don't Call It Love: Recovery from Sexual Addiction, Patrick Carnes, Ph.D., Bantam, 1991

Sex God: Exploring the Endless Connections between Sexuality and Spirituality, Rob Bell, Zondervan, 2007

Flesh: An Unbreakable Habit of Purity in a Pornographic World: Men's Edition, Rick James, WSN Press, 2004

Fantasy: An Insatiable Desire for a Satisfying Love: Women's Edition, Betty Blake Churchill, CruPress, 2005

LEADERS GUIDE TO DISCUSSION QUESTIONS

As the leader, keep in mind that the goal of the time is not to get through every question but to have an engaging discussion. If that's happening, it's likely you will not get through every question, and that's quite all right. Look through the questions in advance to make sure you do get to the ones you feel would be most helpful for the group to discuss.

Publicity to promote this discussion group can be downloaded at www. pornnation.org.

Porn Comes of Age

The focus of this study is considering one's personal sexual history.

1. Discuss.

2. Discuss.

3. Discuss.

4. Women are objects; violence and rape are acceptable sexual preferences; etc.

5. Discuss.

6. Discuss.

7. It might be interesting to raise the issue of double standards: we often have moral expectations for parents that we don't have for ourselves— why is that?

8. You might want to let the group know you're available to talk later if there is something a member really wants or needs to share in private.

9. You probably want to share your own experience first to break the ice on this question.

10. Discuss.

11. Don't squelch discussion with the right answer, but the right answer is, of course, that God does not like porn—God created sex and is saddened by the abuse and exploitation of it.

12. Discuss.

Married to Porn

This study considers the effects of sex and porn in relationships.

1. Discuss.

2. Discuss.

3. Discuss.

4. You're not looking for a right answer here. Allow people to share.

5. These may vary by sex, but there is no definitive answer.

6. You may want to share first to break the ice on this question.

7. Discuss.

8. Discuss. I've found that if it's justifiable for any reason, you'll find a reason to justify it.

9. Obviously affairs, sexual dissatisfaction, and porn play a role; *how much* of a role they play is worth discussing.

10. Discuss.

11. On this question it would be helpful for you to share your spiritual story and perspective.

12. From a Christian perspective, both mirror the relationship found among the members of the Trinity. In sex and marriage there is "oneness," while at the same time plurality. Marriage is also a living metaphor for God's relationship with His people. You might cite Ephesians 5:25–30 to show the connection between marriage and our relationship with God, or perhaps a more interesting passage making the same point through a negative example is the first few verses of Hosea, where God asks Hosea to marry a prostitute to mirror how Israel has behaved in their relationship with God.

13. In marriage you belong to each other. If someone had sex with your wife or husband before marriage, in essence someone was stealing from you, taking what should ultimately be yours alone.

Generation Sex

The focus of this study is sex and porn as it relates to our culture.

1. Discuss.

2. Discuss.

3. Among other things, sexual involvement, as well as dressing and acting sexual or sexy at a much younger age.

4. Discuss.

5. Interestingly, they are often perceived with the same scandal that the promiscuous experienced a generation ago. It might be worth noting this fact, as the point is to observe how quickly the sexual environment is changing. I honestly think that in today's world, virgins receive more ridicule than I do as a sex addict.

6. Discuss.

7. Listen to the reasons and ask if those same reasons might not be true even for the ages of 14–18.

8. It might be good to point out how easy it is to rationalize our behavior.

9. I think there's little doubt that porn objectifies women. Why women participate is complicated: sometimes for very tragic reasons (drugs, the sex trade, abuse), sometimes not for very good reasons at all.

10. I think for a Christian this is much easier to answer, as the Scriptures provide clear guidelines. Without a standard like the Bible, drawing lines becomes arbitrary.

11. While not negating psychological factors, sexual deviancy, in my mind, is strong evidence of our sinful nature. There is clearly an attraction to things simply *because* they are bent. As our souls are perverted to worship other things besides God, so too are our minds, which experience attraction to things we were not created to be attracted to. Romans 1:24–28 is a very powerful description of the process of moral and sexual deviation, although raising the issue of homosexuality may elicit strong reactions.

12. Typically, issues of where to draw the line; the question of what constitutes "art" versus pornography; and who decides what should be censored.

13. You're looking for things like: waiting for sex until marriage is outdated; homosexuality is natural; a person's worth is determined by their appearance, etc.

14. Discuss.

15. Discuss.

Sex Syndrome

The topic is the addictive and progressive nature of sex and porn obsession.

1. Discuss.

2. A growing appetite for sexual stimuli; a desire for increasingly graphic depictions of sexuality; increased feelings of compulsiveness; crossing lines of behavior.

3. Discuss. When it comes to Internet pornography, many have feelings of compulsivity. This may be especially true for Christians who are part of a small minority who actually try to refrain from viewing it. You don't tend to experience such feelings unless you are trying *not* to do something.

4. You might want to share first to get the conversation going.

5. Anything that creates "feel good" chemistry in the brain and body is potentially addictive.

6. Typically, the ability to control the behavior is the indicator, including the freedom to refrain from doing it.

7. Guilt tends to involve feeling bad for something you've done, while shame is deeper: feeling bad about who you are. Being sexually abused, for example, causes great shame even though the victim did nothing wrong.

8. Discuss.

9. I think this is clearly the case. Biological, familial, and psychological factors do make people more susceptible.

10. Discuss. I think it can. There is a line to walk between understanding a person's condition and situation and excusing their behavior, as if they had no choice in the matter. It's important to know why we do things; it's also important to take responsibility for our actions.

11. Often, addicts' feelings of powerlessness cause them to realize that they lack the moral capacity to simply stop the behavior. Addicts both want to do the action as well as not do it; they cannot rescue themselves from their situation—*they* are the problem.

12. Discuss.

13. Discuss.

14. It would be important for you to share your spiritual journey and how you came to faith, perhaps even being willing to stay after and talk more about it with whoever might be interested.

Which Way to Redemption?

This study looks at God's role in making us well.

1. Religion can be just another list of dos and don'ts, bringing guilt when standards are broken and providing neither absolution nor the power to change. A greater awareness of the good can be just a greater awareness of guilt.

2. Pray, try harder, stop doing it.

3. If redemption or salvation hinges on our moral performance, no one could be very hopeful of ever achieving it. Even if "not lusting" were the only requirement, who could be hopeful of redemption? (Matthew 5:28; Romans 2:21–23)

4. Religion tells you what must be done in order to be redeemed, so in that sense it is a map or path to redemption, not redemption itself.

5. Discuss.

6. Christ forgives our sins by dying for them. Redemption lies in what He has done for us, not in our moral track record. (Romans 5:8)

7. Sex functions best within the unconditional love of a marriage relationship. Following this prescription protects us from any number of negative consequences: sexually transmitted diseases, jealousy, shame, low self-esteem, emotional scars, etc. In the end, it provides the most fulfilling sex life possible in a sinful world. (1 Peter 1:15–16; 1 Thessalonians 4:4–7)

8. Christ pays for our sins; we do not earn salvation. It is a gift. We are also credited with Christ's righteousness, and God empowers us to change, not leaving it to our willpower alone. These are all things done for us by Christ earning our redemption; they can't be achieved through our efforts or determination. (Ephesians 2:8–9; Colossians 1:11–14)

9. His life had been built around his disability—it was who he was, what he did for a living. "Getting well" involved a change of life, not just the healing, and he may not have wanted a complete change of life.

10. Being healthy sexually often requires a radical change of lifestyle, and in coming to Christ we are not just agreeing to accept His forgiveness, but surrendering our lives to Him to change and lead. (1 Corinthians 6:18–20; 1 Peter 2:24)

11. After people write down their list, read through the reflection section. You, again, might share your own personal story to help others understand this decision. If appropriate, you should provide an opportunity to pray right then and there. If not, suggest that they might do so on their own that evening.

As this is the last study, you should ask if the group would like to continue meeting. You've created a community, and it would be sad to end it. Depending on the group's needs, you may wish to delve deeper into a biblical study of sex (see Small Group Resources above), turn to spiritual growth topics, or study a book of the Bible.